W9-ANI-575

WITHDRAWN

WITHDRAWN

BONNIE
B L A I R

WITHDRAWN

(Photo on front cover.)

Bonnie Blair at full speed during the women's 500 meter at the World Speed Skating Championships.

(Photo on previous pages.)

Blair takes fourth place in the 1,500 meter event at Hamar, Norway.

Text copyright © 1996 by The Child's World, Inc.
All rights reserved. No part of this book may be reproduced
or utilized in any form or by any means without written
permission from the Publisher.
Printed in the United States of America.

Photography supplied by Wide World Photos Inc.

Library of Congress Cataloging-in-Publication Data
Rambeck, Richard.
Bonnie Blair / Richard Rambeck.
p. cm.
Summary: Relates the speed skating accomplishments
of the winner of five gold medals in three Olympics, the
most by any United States female athlete in history.
ISBN 1-56766-186-6 (lib. bdg.)
1. Blair, Bonnie. 1964- —Juvenile literature.
2. Skaters—United States—Biography—Juvenile literature.
3. Speed skating—United States—Juvenile literature.
[1. Blair, Bonnie, 1964- 2. Ice skaters. 3. Women—
Biography 4. Speed skating.]
I. Title
GV850.B63R36 1995   95-6464
796.332'092 B—dc20   CIP
                                               AC

BONNIE
B L A I R

BY RICHARD RAMBECK

38212002091020
Main Child Biography
jB
B635r
Rambeck, Richard
Bonnie Blair

RODMAN PUBLIC LIBRARY

*Bonnie Blair
wins the
women's 500
meters at the
1994 Winter
Olympics.*

What more could Bonnie Blair do as a speed skater? She had just won two gold medals at the 1994 Winter Olympics in Norway. In all, she had captured five gold medals in three Olympics, the most by any U.S. female athlete in history. There was no doubt Bonnie Blair was the best speed skater this country had ever produced, but there was one thing she wanted to do before she hung up her skates. She wanted to skate 500 meters in less than 39 seconds.

In 1988, at the Winter Olympics in Calgary, Canada, Blair had almost broken the 39-second mark. In the finals of the 500 meters, she crossed the finish line in a world record 39.10 seconds. It was Blair's first Olympic gold medal, but she wanted to skate faster. She wanted to break 39 seconds, which to speed skaters is what the four-minute mile was to runners. One month after the Norway Olympics, Blair got her chance to be the fastest skater ever.

The start of a new record in the 500 meters.

Blair entered a 500 meter event in Calgary, on the same rink where she had won her first Olympic gold six years before. She skated as hard as she could for the record. "I knew," she said after the race, "as soon as I crossed the finish line it was a world record." It was: 38.99 seconds. Blair now had five gold medals and an unofficial title

Blair flashes five fingers to represent her fifth gold medal.

as the fastest woman speed skater ever. It couldn't have happened to a nicer person.

"Bonnie doesn't know she's a celebrity," said Eleanor Blair, Bonnie's mother. "She sees herself as a regular person." Bonnie is a regular person, but she's a person who might just be the best speed skater of all time. If she were, say, a male basketball player who was the best in the world, Blair would make millions of dollars every year. Blair, however, is a speed skater, and speed skaters aren't worried about how much money they'll make from their sport.

"We do it because we love what we're doing," said Blair, whose brothers and sisters also were speed skaters. "I never in my wildest dreams would have thought I would accomplish what I have in the sport. I never got into it to make money." No, she didn't make a lot of money, but she won a lot of Olympic medals (six, including five golds and one bronze). She also won a lot of awards—honors rarely given to speed skaters.

In December 1994, Blair was named Sportswoman of the Year by *Sports Illustrated* magazine. Soon after, the U.S. Olympic Committee voted her

Blair waves after completing her heat in the women's 1,000 meters.

Sportswoman of the Year for 1994. Finally, the Associated Press honored Blair as the Female Athlete of the Year. "When she retires," said her coach, Nick Thometz, "she will have been on top from 1988 to 1995. That's because of her work habits and lifestyle. She's the same person she was before her success."

Bonnie Blair began speed skating at the age of two, using hand-me-down skates from her older brothers and sisters. Growing up in Champaign, Illinois, Blair skated on the indoor rink at the University of Illinois. She loved to skate, but she also loved to do other things. By the time she got to high school, Blair was a skater, a good student, and a cheerleader, and she was also active in student government.

Blair takes a third in Ikaho, Japan in 1993.

Blair knew she needed to spend more time skating if she was to realize her dream of competing in the Olympics. "Bonnie dedicated her whole life to skating," said her older sister Mary, who herself was a national senior speed skating champion. In 1984, Bonnie raised $37,000 by herself to fund a trip to Europe so she could train for the 1984 Olympics. She competed in the 500 meters in those Olympics and finished eighth.

Four years later, Blair was back at the Olympics, which were held in Calgary. She won the 500 meters in a world-record time. Four years after that, she won both the 500 and 1,000 meters at the Winter Olympics in Albertville, France. Finally, in 1994, Blair captured both the 500 and 1,000 meters at the Olympics in Norway. Then, for the "thrill of competition," she entered the 1,500 meters and finished fourth.

When the 1994 Winter Olympics ended, Blair was the proud owner of more gold medals than any other U.S. woman, but she hadn't changed a bit. Success hadn't spoiled

Bonnie Blair. "All I hear about her are nice things," said her brother Rob. "She's a special person. There's not much more I can say, but I'm real proud of her." Rob is proud of his sister, but he's also inspired by her many achievements.

S ince 1987, Rob Blair has had a brain tumor that doctors can't operate on. He often suffers seizures that leave him temporarily unable to use many muscles on the right side of his body. Rob draws a lot of strength from his sister. "I watch what Bonnie does, and that just feeds into me. She has said that I've inspired her, and that's nice of

Blair celebrates after winning the 500 meter event at the 1992 Winter Olympics.

her to say. But I've gotten a lot more from her than the other way around."

In March 1995, Bonnie Blair, not quite 31 years old, retired from speed skating. She concluded probably the most remarkable career of any U.S. women athlete. Blair had met three U.S. presidents, she had served as grand marshal of the Indianapolis 500, and she had been honored during Chicago Bulls and Chicago Cubs home games. She was simply the best and the fastest U.S. women speed skater ever — and, despite her success, she never changed.